Hacer gráficas/
Making Graphs

Tableros de conteo
Tally Charts

por/by Vijaya Khisty Bodach

CAPSTONE PRESS
a capstone imprint

A+ Books are published by Capstone Press,
1710 Roe Crest Drive, North Mankato, Minnesota 56003.
www.capstonepub.com

Library of Congress Cataloging-in-Publication Data
Bodach, Vijaya.
 [Tally charts. Spanish & English]
 Tableros de conteo / por Vijaya Khisty Bodach = Tally charts / by vijaya Khisty Bodach.
   p. cm.—(A+ bilingüe. Hacer gráficas = Bilingual. Making graphs)
 Includes bibliographical references and index.
 Summary: "Uses simple text and photographs to describe how to make and use tally
charts—in both English and Spanish"—Provided by publisher.
 ISBN 978-1-4296-6103-4 (library binding)
 ISBN 978-1-4296-8546-7 (paperback)
 1. Mathematics—Graphic methods—Juvenile literature. 2. Mathematics—Charts,
diagrams, etc.—Juvenile literature. 3. Tallies—Juvenile literature. I. Title. II. Title:
Tally charts.
 QA40.5.B64218 2011
 510—dc22   2010042252

Editorial Credits

Heather Adamson, editor; Strictly Spanish, translation services; Juliette Peters, designer;
    Eric Manske, bilingual book designer; Wanda Winch, media researcher; Kelly Garvin,
    photo stylist; Sarah Bennett, production specialist

Photo Credits

All photos Capstone Press/Karon Dubke, except page 20 Shutterstock/oksanaperkins, page 28
    iStockphoto, and page 29 Shutterstock/Raymond Kasprzak

Note to Parents, Teachers, and Librarians

Hacer gráficas/Making Graphs uses color photographs and a nonfiction format to introduce
readers to graphing concepts in both English and Spanish. *Tableros de conteo/Tally Charts*
is designed to be read aloud to a pre-reader, or to be read independently by an early reader.
Images and activities encourage mathematical thinking in early readers and listeners. The book
encourages further learning by including the following sections: Table of Contents, Glossary,
Internet Sites, and Index. Early readers may need assistance using these features.

Printed in the United States of America.
2593

Table of Contents

Tabla de contenidos

Try to pick up a stick without moving the pile.
How many sticks will each player pick?

Trata de levantar un palito sin mover la pila.
¿Cuántos palitos levantará cada jugador?

We can use tally marks to keep score.
Write the name of each player on a paper.

Nosotros podemos usar marcas de conteo para anotar el puntaje. Escribe el nombre de cada jugador en una hoja de papel.

Line up their sticks next to their names.
Sam picks two sticks before wiggling
the pile. Put his sticks in a row by his name.

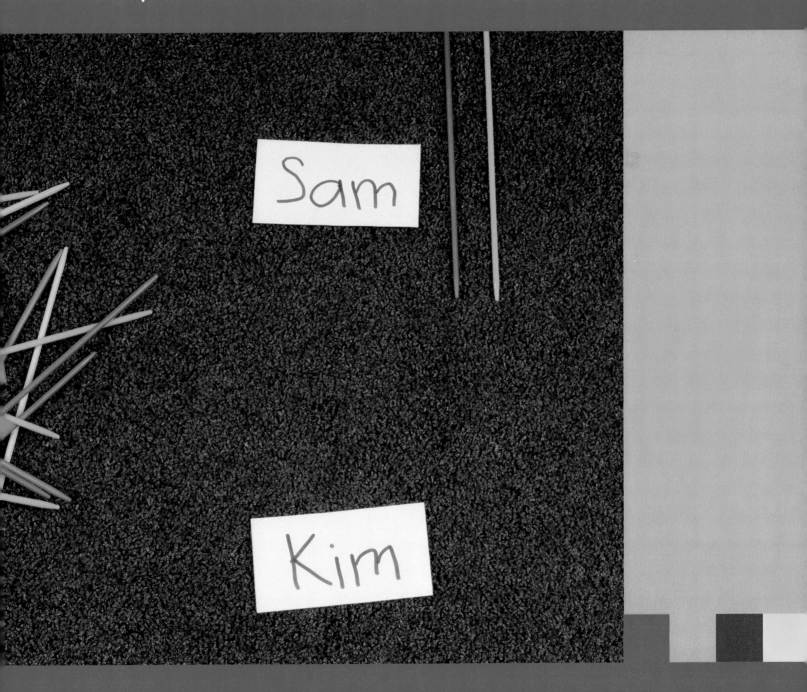

Alinea los palitos de cada jugador junto a su nombre.
Sam levanta dos palitos antes de mover la pila.
Pon sus palitos en una línea junto a su nombre.

Kim grabs five sticks. Tally marks are made in groups of five. The fifth tally mark goes across the other four.

Kim levanta cinco palitos. Las marcas de conteo se hacen en grupos de cinco. La quinta marca de conteo atraviesa las otras cuatro.

Sam's turn again. He picks two more sticks. Kim takes three sticks on her turn.

Es el turno de Sam otra vez. Él levanta dos palitos más. Kim levanta tres palitos cuando es su turno.

Kim is the winner this time.
She scored the most points.

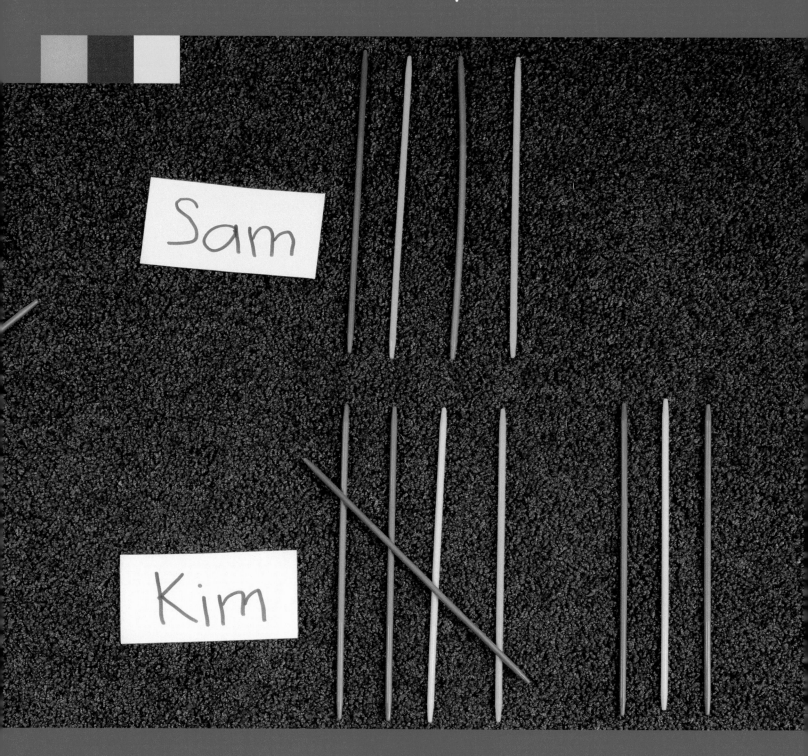

Kim es la ganadora esta vez.
Ella anotó la mayor cantidad de puntos.

We can keep a tally on paper too.
Tallies help us count things as they happen.

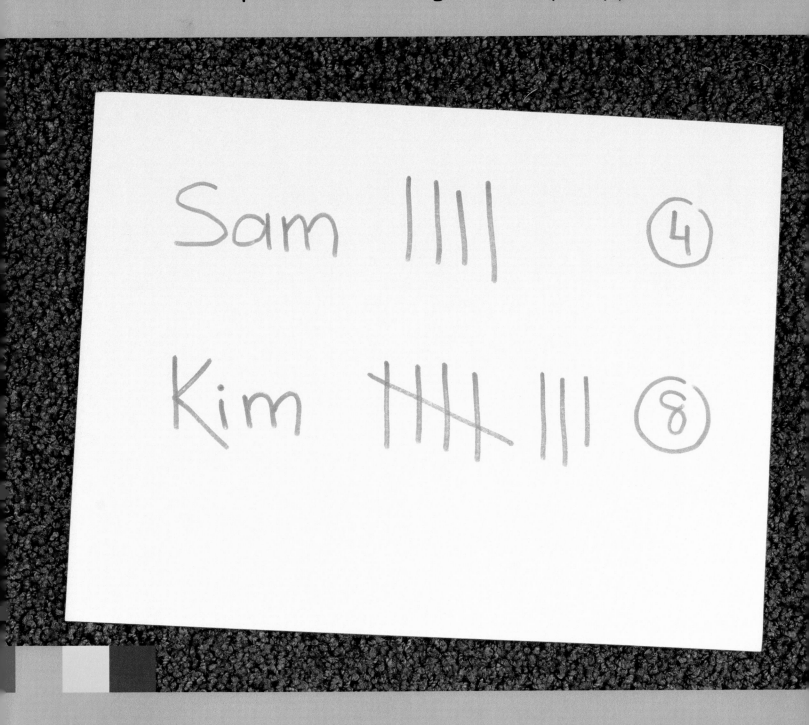

También podemos hacer conteos en papel.
Las marcas de conteo nos ayudan a contar cosas a medida que ocurren.

Tally marks help track favorites. Which flavor of ice cream do people like best?

Las marcas de conteo ayudan a registrar preferencias. ¿Qué sabor de helado es el favorito?

More people like strawberry than vanilla. But chocolate is the favorite.

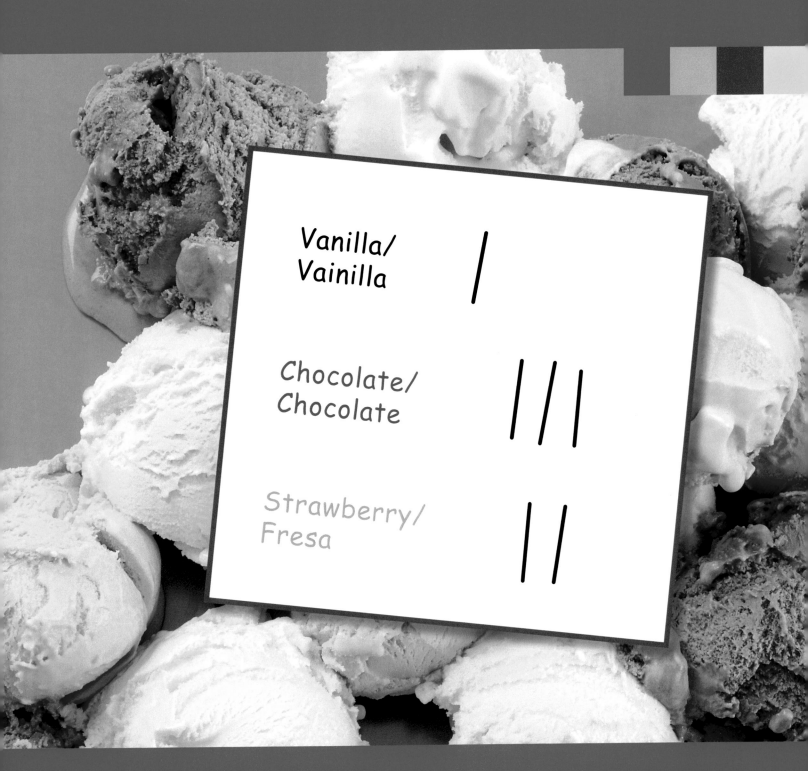

Vanilla/ Vainilla	I
Chocolate/ Chocolate	I I I
Strawberry/ Fresa	I I

Más personas prefieren fresa que vainilla. Pero chocolate es el favorito.

What color toothbrush is most popular?
Make a mark for each brush.

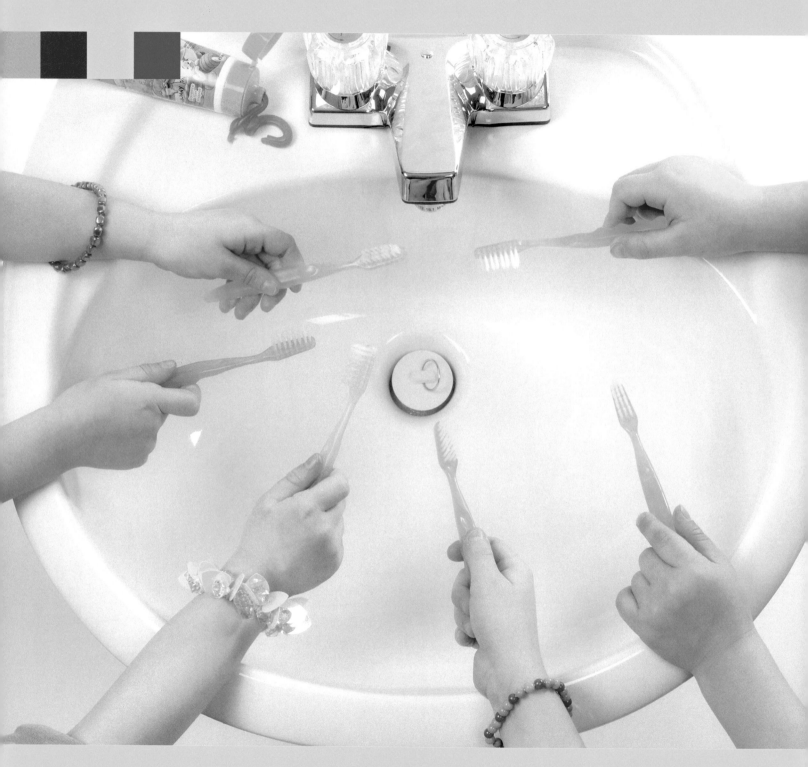

¿Qué color de cepillo de dientes es el más popular?
Haz una marca por cada cepillo.

Green had the most marks. It's more popular than orange or pink.

El verde tiene la mayor cantidad de marcas. Es más popular que el anaranjado o el rosa.

These kids want to play their favorite sports.
Let's take a vote to decide what to play first.

Estos niños quieren jugar a sus deportes favoritos.
Vamos a votar para decidir a qué jugar primero.

Basketball has the most votes. More kids want to play basketball than the other sports.

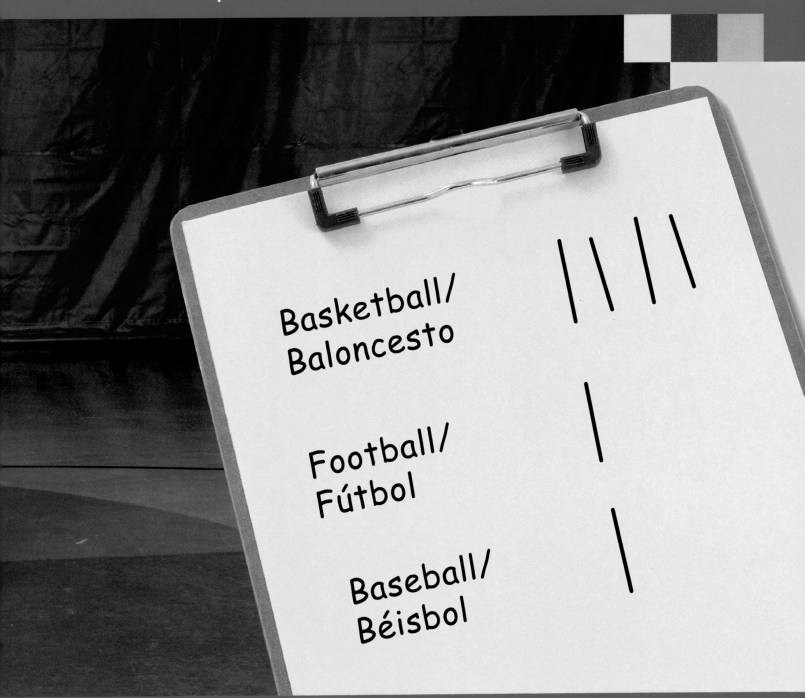

Basketball/
Baloncesto

Football/
Fútbol

Baseball/
Béisbol

El baloncesto tiene la mayor cantidad de votos. Más niños quieren jugar al baloncesto que a los otros deportes.

You can use tallies to count cars on a trip. Write a list of colors. Mark a line each time a car passes.

Red/Rojo |

Green/Verde

Blue/Azul ||

Tú puedes usar marcas de conteo para contar autos en un viaje. Escribe una lista de colores. Haz una marca cada vez que pasa un auto.

A red car goes by. Make a tally mark next to the word red. Next, two blue cars pass.

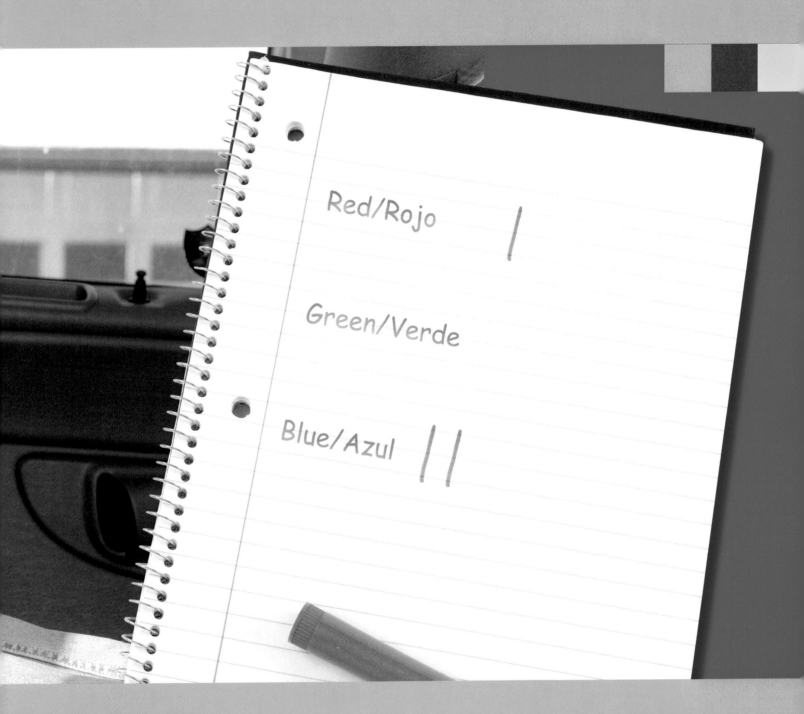

Red/Rojo |

Green/Verde

Blue/Azul | |

Pasa un automóvil rojo. Haz una marca de conteo junto a la palabra rojo. Luego pasan dos automóviles azules.

A couple more red cars zoom on by.
Then two green cars. And three more blue
cars. Keep making tallies for each car.

Un par de autos rojos pasan rápido. Luego
pasan dos autos verdes. Y otros tres autos
azules. Sigue haciendo una marca de conteo
por cada auto.

Count the tallies and write the totals.
We saw more blue cars than red.
We saw the fewest green cars.

Red/Rojo ||| ③

Green/Verde || ②

Blue/Azul || ||| ⑤

Cuenta las marcas y escribe los totales.
Nosotros vimos más autos azules que rojos.
Nosotros vimos menos autos verdes.

We can tally how many free throw baskets each child makes.

Nosotros podemos hacer el conteo de cuántos tiros al cesto acierta cada niño.

Karl made three baskets. Julie made five baskets. Max had the most free throws. He made six baskets!

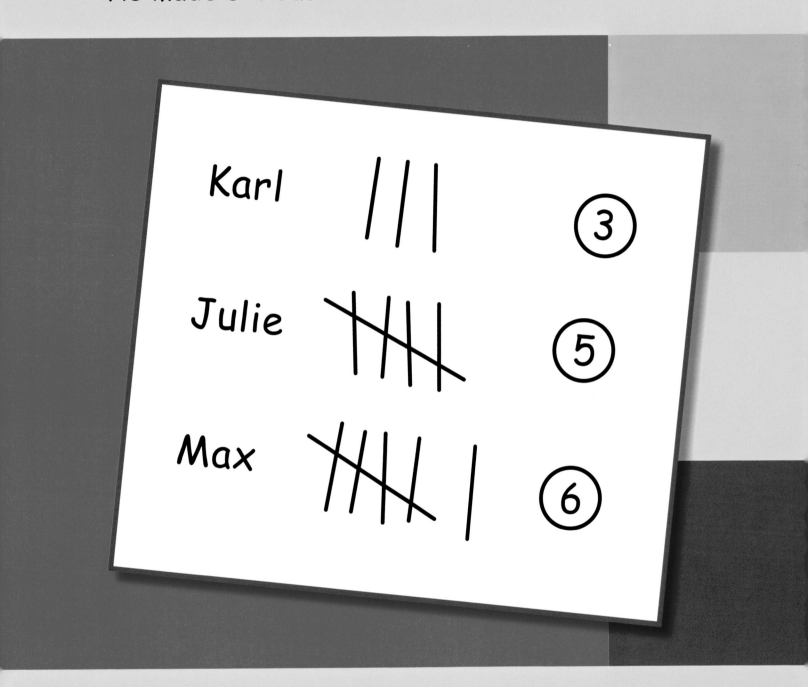

Karl acertó tres tiros. Julie acertó cinco tiros. Max tuvo el número máximo de aciertos. ¡Él acertó seis tiros!

How many coins will land heads up?
Tally marks can help us keep track.

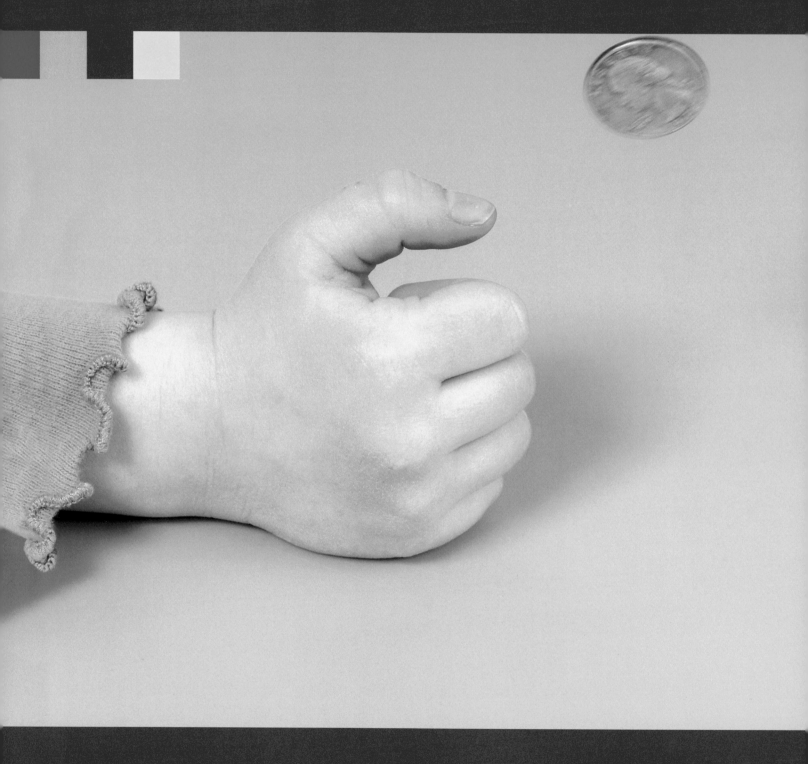

¿Cuántas monedas caerán de cara?
Las marcas de conteo nos ayudan a llevar control.

Seven coins landed heads up.

Siete monedas cayeron de cara.

Let's see how many times the carousel spins each ride. Make a tally mark each time the white horse passes.

Veamos cuántas vueltas da el carrusel en cada juego. Haz una marca de conteo cada vez que pasa el caballo blanco.

White Horse/
Caballo blanco

꜀꜀꜀꜀꜀ ꜀꜀꜀꜀꜀ ꜀꜀

A busy bird feeder is fun to watch. You can use tallies to keep track of the birds.

Un comedero de pájaros con mucha actividad es lindo de ver. Tú puedes usar marcas de conteo para registrar los pájaros.

What type of birds visit each day? When do more birds visit—morning or evening?

¿Qué tipo de pájaros visitan cada día? ¿Cuándo visitan más pájaros, de mañana o de noche?

Glossary

carousel—an amusement ride that turns in circles

chart—to show information in the form of a
   picture or graph

favorite—a thing or person that you like best

tally—a score or record; a tally mark is one straight
   line; tallies is the plural of tally

total—a number gotten by adding up the whole amount

vote—to make a choice

Internet Sites

FactHound offers a safe, fun way to find Internet sites related to this book. All of the sites on FactHound have been researched by our staff.

Here's all you do:

Visit *www.facthound.com*

Type in this code: 9781429661034

Super-cool stuff! Check out projects, games and lots more at
www.capstonekids.com

Glosario

el carrusel—un juego del parque de diversiones que da vuelta en círculos

favorito—una cosa o persona que prefieres

la marca de conteo—una línea recta junto a otra línea recta para llevar un registro

la tabla—para mostrar información en forma de dibujo o gráfica

el total—un número que se obtiene sumando la cantidad entera

votar—hacer una elección

Sitios de Internet

FactHound brinda una forma segura y divertida de encontrar sitios de Internet relacionados con este libro. Todos los sitios en FactHound han sido investigados por nuestro personal.

Esto es todo lo que tienes que hacer:

Visita *www.facthound.com*

Ingresa este código: 9781429661034

¡Algo súper divertido! Hay proyectos, juegos y mucho más en **www.capstonekids.com**

Index

Índice

If I Were an
Astronaut

by Eric Braun   illustrated by Sharon Harmer

Special thanks to our advisers for their expertise:

Joe Tanner
Former Astronaut
Aerospace Engineering Sciences
University of Colorado at Boulder

Terry Flaherty, Ph.D.
Professor of English
Minnesota State University, Mankato

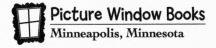

Picture Window Books
Minneapolis, Minnesota

Editor: Shelly Lyons
Designer: Tracy Davies
Page Production: Melissa Kes
Art Director: Nathan Gassman
Editorial Director: Nick Healy
Creative Director: Joe Ewest
The illustrations in this book were created with digital and traditional drawing and painting.

Picture Window Books
1710 Roe Crest Drive
North Mankato, MN 56003
877-845-8392
www.capstonepub.com

Library of Congress Cataloging-in-Publication Data
Braun, Eric, 1971-
If I were an astronaut / by Eric Braun ; illustrated by Sharon Harmer.
p. cm. — (Dream big!)
Includes bibliographical references and index.
ISBN 978-1-4048-5534-2 (library binding)
ISBN 978-1-4048-5710-0 (paperback)
1. Astronauts—Juvenile literature. 2. Astronautics—Juvenile literature. I. Harmer, Sharon, ill. II. Title. TL793.B72 2010
  629.45—dc22   2009006883

If I were an astronaut, I would fly a spacecraft in outer space.

If I were an astronaut, I would feel the G's. Gravity would pin me to my seat as I blasted off. My arms and legs would feel like concrete as I rose into space.

If I were an astronaut, I would dock my ship to the Space Station. I would gently settle the shuttle into place.

Be careful! Lighten up on the thrusters!

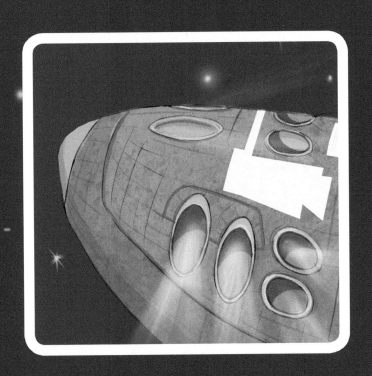

If I were an astronaut, I would be part of a super team. I would work with astronauts and scientists from all around the world. We would learn from each other and help each other. We would have the greatest jobs we could imagine.

If I were an astronaut, I would run a robotic arm. I would lift a huge truss from the shuttle. The part would be added to the Space Station.

Don't bump it! Don't drop it!

The International Space Station is a satellite. It is a place where astronauts take turns living for months at a time. The Space Station continues to grow. Spacecraft launch from Earth with new parts. Parts are handled with a robotic arm.

If I were an astronaut, I would take a space walk. I would fix a section of the Space Station. Stars, planets, and deep space would be all around.

What a view!

If I were an astronaut, I would try to keep my food from floating away! Some food, such as spaghetti or scrambled eggs, would be dried. I would add water before I warmed it in the oven.

15

If I were an astronaut, I would sleep stuck to the wall. My sleeping bag would keep me from drifting around the room. I could even sleep upside-down, like a bat!

If I were an astronaut, I would do cool science experiments. I might even discover important new medicines.

Experiments on crystals in space have taught scientists how to make better medicines and even computer chips.

If I were an astronaut, each day would be an adventure. I would visit outer space and see amazing things. I would live in the Space Station for months at a time.

I would have a blast!

How do you get to be an Astronaut?

People who want to be astronauts study lots of math and science. They get hundreds of hours of experience flying. They exercise a lot, so they are in great shape. People who want to be astronauts have to be patient and believe in themselves. It takes a long time and a lot of work to be an astronaut.

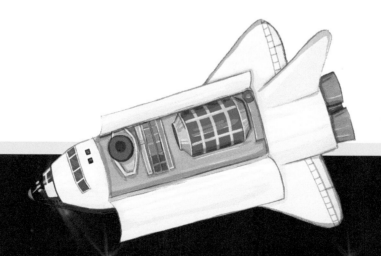

Glossary

dock—to join with

experiments—scientific tests that are used to prove or discover something

G's—short for G-force; this is how acceleration is measured

gravity—the force that pulls objects toward Earth's surface

launch—to send something into outer space

robotic arm—a mechanical arm operated by an astronaut

satellite—a spacecraft that circles around Earth or another body in outer space

shuttle—a spacecraft that takes people and supplies into outer space and back

spacecraft—a vehicle that travels in outer space

Space Station—short for the International Space Station (ISS); the Space Station is a research laboratory that orbits Earth; it is a joint project shared by the space agencies from the United States, Russia, Canada, Japan, and European nations

thrusters—rocket engines that control how a spacecraft moves

truss—a piece of framework that supports the larger structure

To Learn More

More Books to Read

Aldrin, Buzz. *Reaching for the Moon*. New York: Harper Collins, 2005.

Bredeson, Carmen. *What Do Astronauts Do?* Berkeley Heights, N.J.: Enslow Elementary, 2008.

McCarthy, Meghan. *Astronaut Handbook*. New York: Alfred A. Knopf, 2008.

Internet Sites

FactHound offers a safe, fun way to find Internet sites related to this book. All of the sites on FactHound have been researched by our staff.

Here's all you do:

Visit *www.facthound.com*

FactHound will fetch the best sites for you!

Index

Look for all of the books in the Dream Big! series:

If I Were a Ballerina

If I Were a Major League Baseball Player

If I Were an Astronaut

If I Were the President